Guess What

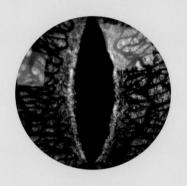

Published in the United States of America by
Cherry Lake Publishing
Ann Arbor, Michigan
www.cherrylakepublishing.com

Reading Adviser: Marla Conn MS, Ed., Literacy specialist, Read-Ability, Inc.
Book Designer: Felicia Macheske

Photo Credits: © Robert Eastman, cover/Shutterstock.com, 3, 21; © Steve Collender/Shutterstock.com, 1, 4; © reptiles4all/
Shutterstock.com, 7; © Hitman1111/Dreamstime.com, 8; © fivespots/Shutterstock.com, 12; © Cathy Keifer/Shutterstock.com, 17;
© Valentina Po/Shutterstock.com, 18; © Andrey_Kuzmin/Shutterstock.com, back cover; © Eric Isselee/Shutterstock.com, back cover:
© Andrey_Kuzmin/Shutterstock.com, back cover

Library of Congress Cataloging-in-Publication Data has been filed and is available at catalog.loc.gov

Cherry Lake Publishing would like to acknowledge the work of The Partnership for 21st Century Skills.
Please visit *www.p21.org* for more information.

Printed in the United States of America
Corporate Graphics

Table of Contents

I see well in the dark.

I have a wide mouth.

8

My skin
feels dry.

And I shed my skin so I can grow.

My tail can break off and grow back.

Sometimes I like to hide.

I eat insects and worms. Yummy!

I was hatched from an egg.

Do you know what I am?

I'm a Gecko!

About Geckos

1. There are many kinds of geckos. Leopard geckos are the most common pet gecko.

2. Leopard geckos can live 15 to 20 years.

3. Most geckos don't have eyelids, but leopard geckos do.

4. Leopard geckos are nocturnal. This means they move around at night.

5. Leopard geckos can make noises like a chirp or small bark.

Things to Think About
Before You Get a Pet

1. Can you take care of a pet for its whole life?

2. Do you have the money and the time to care for a pet?

3. Could you **adopt** a pet from a **rescue shelter**?

4. Do you have space in your home for a pet?

5. Can you keep a pet safe?

6. Can you keep other animals and people safe from a pet?

Glossary

adopt (uh-DOHPT) to bring an animal into your family

hatched (HACHD) came out of an egg as a baby

insects (IN-sekts) small animals with three pairs of legs, one or two pairs of wings, and three main parts to its body

rescue shelter (RES-kyoo SHEL-tur) a place where an animal that was in danger or was not wanted can stay

shed (SHED) to lose

Index